AFRICAN AMERICAN ASTRONAUTS
& SPACE PIONEERS

AFRICAN AMERICAN ASTRONAUTS
& SPACE PIONEERS

T.M. Moody

African American Astronauts & Space Pioneers
African American History for Kids, #3

Copyright © 2022 T.M. Moody

All rights reserved. No part of this book may be reproduced or transmitted in any form or by any means without written permission of the publisher. For questions, contact us at info@thekulturekidz.com or visit our website at thekulturekidz.com for printables already designated for noncommercial use.

Paperback ISBN: 979-8814115621

Kulture Kidz Books
Tymm Publishing LLC
www.tymmpublishing.com

Author: T.M. Moody
Editor: editorsylvia
Illustrations: johangerrar
Cover and Interior Designer: TywebbinCreations.com

Table of Contents

Introduction	3
Part 1: Space Pioneers	7
Mary Jackson	9
Katherine Johnson	13
Dorothy Vaughan	17
Melba Roy Mouton	21
Christine Darden	25
Robert H. Lawrence	29
Part 2: Space Shuttle ERA	33
Guion Bluford	35
Ronald E. McNair	39
Frederick Gregory	43
Charles Bolden	47
Mae C. Jemison	51
Stephanie D. Wilson	55
Michael P. Anderson	59
Joan Higginbotham	63
Part 3: Future of Spaceflight	67
Victor Glover	69
Dr. Sian Proctor	73
Jessica Watkins	77
Timeline	81

Glossary	87
Activity Book	91
About the Author	93
Kulture Kidz Books	95

Introduction

Have you ever dreamed of going into space? Maybe you're a fan of science fiction like Star Wars or Star Trek. Humans traveling and living in space has been going on since the late 1950s.

There have been many African Americans who have been important to the launch of space programs in the United States.

This book is split into three parts:

Astronaut Buzz Aldrin on the moon. NASA Public Domain

Part 1–The Space Race

Meet space pioneers who were behind the scenes at the National Aeronautics and Space Administration (NASA) during the Space Race. The Space Race was a major competition between the United States and the Soviet Union to see which one would become the first in space. This competition took place between 1957 and 1969.

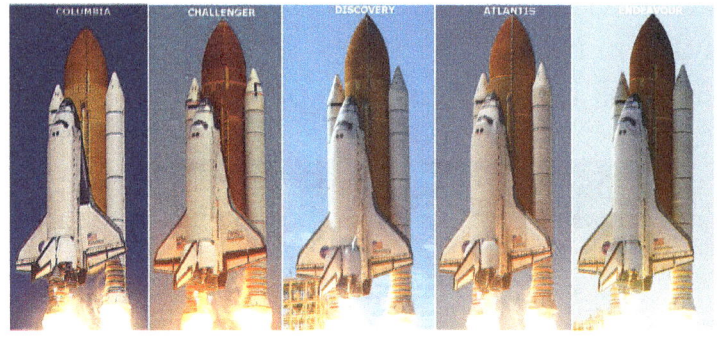

NASA space shuttle fleet. NASA Public Domain

Part 2–Space Shuttle Era

Meet African American astronauts, both men and women, who have flown in space during the Space Shuttle Era. From April 12, 1981 to July 21, 2011, NASA's space shuttle fleet included *Columbia*, *Challenger*, *Discovery*, *Atlantis* and *Endeavour*. These space shuttles flew 135 missions and were used to build the International Space Station.

Astronaut Jessica Watkins of NASA's Commercial Crew Program, SpaceX Crew-4 Mission Specialist, poses for a portrait in her pressure suit at SpaceX headquarters in Hawthorne, California. Credit: SpaceX

Part 3–Future of Spaceflight

When the Space Shuttles retired in 2011, NASA began working with private companies like SpaceX to build the next spacecrafts. Meet African American astronauts and a civilian who have flown on the newest vehicles for space travel.

PART 1

SPACE PIONEERS

MARY JACKSON

1921-2005

Mary Winston Jackson was an American mathematician and aerospace engineer at NASA.

Mary Winston was born on April 9, 1921, in Hampton, Virginia. She excelled in school and graduated with honors from George P. Phenix Training School.

In 1942, Mary earned a bachelor's degree in mathematics and physical science from Hampton Institute (now Hampton University). After she graduated, Mary taught math for a year before becoming a bookkeeper at the National Catholic Community Center. In 1951, NACA recruited Mary and she worked as a "human computer" at Langley Research Center in Hampton, Virginia. She would work beside other women like Katherine Jackson and Dorothy Vaughan, her supervisor, in the West Area Computing Unit. Even though the African American women in this unit helped with the complex math problems, they had to be **segregated** from the white workers. That meant they worked in separate areas and used separate bathrooms and cafeterias.

In 1953, Mary began working for a NASA engineer named Kazimierz Czarnecki. She worked on the Supersonic Pressure Tunnel, which was a wind tunnel. Engineers would create winds almost at the speed of sound (super fast!) and study how the forces (the push or pull) affected the model inside the wind tunnel. Her boss, Czarnecki, thought

Mary would make a great engineer. After some difficulties, Mary could finally take graduate level math and physics courses at The University of Virginia. She got her degree in aerospace engineering and became NASA's first African American engineer in 1958.

Mary continued to work as an engineer at NASA until she retired in 1985.

Mary Jackson was featured in the movie, *Hidden Figures*, in 2016. Actress and singer, Janelle Monáe played her.

KATHERINE JOHNSON

1918-2020

Katherine Johnson, a mathematician, is one of the first African-American women to work as a NASA scientist.

Katherine Johnson was born on August 26, 1918, in White Sulphur Springs, West Virginia. Her teachers noticed she had very strong math skills. When she was ten years old, Katherine's family enrolled her in a special high school. The school was located on the West Virginia State College campus.

When Katherine graduated from high school, she began attending West Virginia State. In 1937, Katherine graduated with degrees in mathematics and French. She was only eighteen years old.

She taught math for a few years before hearing about an opportunity with the National Advisory Committee for Aeronautics (NACA). They were hiring African American mathematicians. Katherine officially began working in 1953 alongside other women like Mary Jackson and Dorothy Vaughan. She worked in the West Computing Unit until 1958, when NASA replaced NACA.

After 1958, Katherine worked at NASA as an aerospace technologist. She became very good at calculating the **trajectory** or path needed for an orbital flight. On May 5, 1961, Alan Shepard would become the first American in space thanks to Katherine's calculations. During her career, she also provided calculations to help with the Apollo Moon landing and the start of the Space Shuttle program.

Katherine retired from NASA in 1986, but her role and legacy became more widely known after the *Hidden Figures* movie was released in 2016. Actress Taraji P. Henson played Katherine.

She passed away at the age of 101 on February 24, 2020.

DOROTHY VAUGHAN

1910-2008

Dorothy Vaughan was a mathematician and NASA's first African-American manager.

Dorothy Vaughan was born September 20, 1910, in Kansas City, Missouri. Her family moved to West Virginia when Dorothy was seven years old. An excellent student throughout school, Dorothy graduated as class valedictorian, the top student in her entire class.

In 1929, she graduated from Wilberforce University with a bachelor of arts degree in mathematics. She started her career as a math teacher. There weren't a lot of jobs that an African American could work during her time, but things began to change. NACA needed a lot of mathematicians, also known as "human computers." Dorothy stopped being a teacher and began working at Langley Memorial Aeronautical Laboratory in 1943.

She and her co-workers, Katherine Johnson and Mary Jackson, worked together in the West Computing Unit. Dorothy received a promotion in 1949, becoming the first African American manager at NASA. As a supervisor, Dorothy stood up for her fellow female "human computers" and gained the trust of many of the white employees. She would manage West Computing for almost ten years until NASA shut the division down.

She remained working at NASA until 1971.

In 2016, Dorothy Vaughan was also featured in the movie, *Hidden Figures*. Actress Octavia Spencer played Dorothy.

MELBA ROY MOUTON

1929-1990

Melba Roy Mouton was the Assistant Chief of Research Programs at NASA's Trajectory and Geodynamics Division and headed the group of NASA mathematicians called "human computers".

In 1929, Melba Roy Mouton was born in Fairfax, Virginia. Melba developed a love for math. When she graduated from Manassas Regional High School, she attended Howard University. Melba graduated with a bachelor's degree and later a Master's degree in mathematics from Howard.

Her first job was with the government, where she used her math skills for statistics. **Statistics** involves gathering information, summarizing it, and then deciding what it means. For one of Melba's jobs, she studied the **population,** which is the number of people living in an area like a country, city, or town. She used what she learned to work out plans for the building of future neighborhoods.

In 1959, Melba began working for NASA. She served as Head Mathematician on the Echo Project. Echo 1 was one of the first satellites. A **satellite** can be a moon, planet, or object that **orbits** or moves along a curved path around another planet or a star. The moon is known as a natural satellite, and it orbits around the Earth. The Earth orbits around the Sun, which is the largest star in our universe. Echo 1 and later Echo 2 were artificial satellites that helped with communication here on Earth.

During the 1960s, she was Assistant Chief of Research Programs at NASA's Trajectory and

Geodynamics Division. Melba managed other "human computers" like Mary Jackson, Katherine Johnson, and Dorothy Vaughan.

In the 1970s, Melba continued working at NASA. She learned and taught A Programming Language, also known as APL, one of the oldest programming languages today.

Melba retired from NASA in 1973 and lived in Silver Spring, Maryland, until she passed away in 1990.

CHRISTINE DARDEN

1942-

Christine Mann Darden was one of the few African American female aerospace engineers at NASA.

Christine Darden was born on September 10, 1942, in Monroe, North Carolina. As a child, she had a passion for learning how things worked. After graduating from high school, she attended Hampton Institute. Christine earned a bachelor's degree in math and started her career as a math teacher. Later, she earned a master's degree in applied mathematics at Virginia State University.

In 1967, Christine started her career at NASA as a human computer. As a child, Christine had always loved figuring out how things worked. One day, she asked her supervisor if she could work as an engineer instead. She became one of the few African American female aerospace engineers.

Her main assignment was creating a computer program for sonic boom. A **sonic boom** happens when an object moves faster than the speed of sound, making a really loud sound similar to thunder. Christine's job was to learn how to make the sound boom not so loud. Her twenty-five years of work would help NASA launch quiet but super fast planes known as X-planes in 2016.

In 1983, Christine continued her education by attending George Washington University and earned a doctorate degree in mechanical engineering. After working at NASA for forty years, Christine retired in 2007.

In 2019, Christine was awarded a Congressional Gold Medal for her scientific contributions. Other human computers like Mary Jackson, Katherine Johnson, and Dorothy Vaughan also received this same award that year too.

ROBERT H. LAWRENCE

1935-1967

Major Robert H. Lawrence, Jr. was the first African American selected for the United States space program.

Robert H. Lawrence was born on October 2, 1935, in Chicago, Illinois. He graduated from high school early at sixteen. He also started his Air Force career by participating in the Reserve Officer Training Corps (ROTC). By the time Robert turned twenty years old, he'd received a bachelor's degree in chemistry from Bradley University.

With dreams of becoming a pilot, Robert attended flight training school at Malden Air Force Base. He clocked 2,500 flying hours, with 2,000 of those hours being in jet planes. While learning how to fly, Robert continued his education. In 1965, he earned a Ph.D. in physical chemistry from Ohio State University.

In 1967, Robert became a test pilot at Edwards Air Force Base. They assigned him to the Manned Orbiting Laboratory or MOL Program. While testing a jet plane called a Starfighter, Robert lost his life in December 1967. After the tragedy, the Air Force stopped the MOL Program. Because of the secret nature of the MOL Program, it would be many years before the world knew about Ronald's achievements.

In 1997, almost thirty years after his death, NASA finally recognized Major Robert H. Lawrence, Jr. as the **first African American astronaut**.

Robert's short career of testing jet planes provided the research needed to help scientists bring future space shuttles safely back from orbit.

PART 2
SPACE SHUTTLE ERA

GUION BLUFORD

1942 -

Guion Stewart Bluford Jr. is the first African American astronaut to go to space. He is also a retired U.S. Air Force officer and fighter pilot.

Guion Bluford was born in Philadelphia, Pennsylvania, on November 22, 1942.

In 1964, he received a bachelor of science degree in aerospace engineering from the Pennsylvania State University. After graduation, Guion became a pilot in the Air Force. As a fighter pilot, he flew 144 combat missions during the Vietnam War. Guion worked as an instructor pilot at Sheppard Air Force Base in Texas from 1967 to 1972.

In 1974, Guion earned a master's degree in aerospace engineering. In 1978, he earned a Ph.D. in aerospace engineering and laser physics from the Air Force Institute of Technology.

Also, in 1978, Guion was selected as an astronaut candidate. Almost 8,000 people applied to the program, and Guion was one of thirty-five selected. Included in this group of thirty-five were two other African Americans men, Dr. Ronald McNair and Lt. Col. Fredrick Gregory.

Guion's first mission would be in 1983 on the Space Shuttle *Challenger*. A **space shuttle** is a spacecraft used to transport people and cargo between Earth and space. The mission involved placing an Indian communications satellite in space. This would be the first launch and landing of a space shuttle at night. It also was the first time an African American man went to space.

In 1985, Guion flew on the Space Suttle *Challenger* again, this time as a part of the STS-61A crew. The mission took place in the German D-1 Spacelab.

Guion's final spaceflight was in 1992 on the Space Shuttle *Discovery*. He'd logged over 700 hours in orbit on the *Challenger* and *Discovery*.

In 1993, Bluford resigned from the Air Force and NASA, but he continued to work in the aerospace industry in several leadership positions.

RONALD E. MCNAIR

1950-1986

Astronaut and physicist Dr. Ronald Erwin McNair became the second African American to enter space. He died during the 1986 launch of the Space Shuttle Challenger along with a crew of seven.

Ronald McNair was born in Lake City, South Carolina, on October 21, 1950. He has a famous story that's been told by his brother. At nine years old, Ronald sat at the Lake City Library counter, and he would not leave until the librarian gave him his books. The South was **segregated** when Ronald was a boy. People had to remain separate because of differences like the color of their skin. Even though the police were called, Ronald left the library with his mother and brother and with the books he felt he should be able to read. This determination would remain with Ronald as he excelled in school.

In 1971, he graduated with a Bachelor of Science degree in Physics from North Carolina A&T State University. In 1976, he earned a Ph.D. in LASER Physics at the Massachusetts Institute of Technology or MIT.

In 1978, Ronald was selected as an astronaut candidate. Almost 8,000 people applied to the program, and Ronald was one of thirty-five selected. Included in this group of thirty-five were two other African American men, Guion Bluford and Lt. Col. Fredrick Gregory.

After he completed his training, in August 1979, McNair received his first assignment as a mission specialist astronaut on Space Shuttle flight crews.

Ronald would take his first spaceflight on Space Shuttle *Challenger* in 1984.

During this flight, Ronald's crew member and fellow astronaut Bruce McCandless became the first person to perform a spacewalk without being tethered to a spacecraft. Ronald operated the shuttle's robotic arm that moved the platform where Bruce stood. They would use this process in later space shuttle missions.

In January 1985, Ronald was assigned to the Space Shuttle *Challenger*. This mission included carrying a small satellite, the Spartan Halley. This satellite would observe **Halley's Comet** as it approached the Sun. A comet is a large object made of dust and ice that orbits the Sun. Halley's Comet is one of the few comets that human eyes can see every 75-76 years. Ronald and one of his colleagues would use the robotics arm to bring the Spartan Halley back after the satellite recorded Halley's Comet.

Sadly, on January 28, 1986, the NASA Space Shuttle *Challenger* mission ended in tragedy when the shuttle exploded 73 seconds after takeoff. The entire crew of seven died.

Ronald McNair's name has been honored over the years, including at the segregated library he visited as a young boy. In 2011, they renamed the Lake City Library the Dr. Ronald E. McNair Life History Center.

FREDERICK GREGORY

1941-

Frederick D. Gregory was an astronaut, and he was the first African American deputy administrator at NASA.

Frederick D. Gregory was born in Washington, D.C., in 1941.

In 1964, Frederick received a Bachelor of Science degree from the U.S. Air Force Academy. Soon after graduation, he began helicopter training. As a licensed pilot, he began helicopter rescue missions and served during the Vietnam War. He flew 550 combat rescue missions in Vietnam.

After the war, he served as a missile support helicopter pilot. By 1974, he'd become a test pilot at NASA's Langley Research Center in Virginia. An accomplished pilot, it would be the following year when Frederick would make his transition into spaceflight.

In 1978, Frederick was selected as an astronaut candidate. Almost 8,000 people applied to the program, and Frederick was one of thirty-five selected. Included in this group of thirty-five were two other African Americans men, Guion Bluford and Ronald McNair.

In 1985, Frederick made his first flight into space as the pilot of Space Shuttle *Challenger*. He was the first African American pilot of a spacecraft. There were seven astronauts plus twenty-four rats, and two squirrel monkeys. It wasn't a fun ride but necessary for future research about animals in space. Unfortunately, the cages weren't the best way to transport animals into space. Once the crew and animals adjusted, the mission moved forward.

Frederick had quieter missions, with one making him the first African American space commander. A **commander** is in charge of the crew members and their safety during the flight. His first mission as space commander was with the Space Shuttle *Discovery* in 1989.

The *Discovery* crew were in space on Thanksgiving Day and ate irradiated turkey and freeze-dried vegetables. **Irradiated** means it removed bad things like bacteria and molds to keep the food from going bad. **Freeze-dried** means to dry food in a frozen state under a high vacuum. This keeps the flavor.

After logging in 455 hours in space, Frederick spent the rest of his career at NASA in administrative roles. On August 12, 2002, he became the first African American NASA Deputy Administrator. He remained in this position until 2005.

CHARLES BOLDEN

1946-

Astronaut Charles Frank Bolden, Jr. became the 12th NASA administrator and first African-American administrator in 2009. He served in this position until 2017.

Charles Frank Bolden, Jr. was born in Columbia, South Carolina, on August 19, 1946. After graduating from C. A. Johnson High School, he attended the United States Naval Academy. In 1968, he received a bachelor's degree in electrical science.

Soon after graduating from the U.S. Naval Academy, Charles began his military career in the Marine Corps as a second lieutenant. As a pilot, he flew over 100 combat missions in the Vietnam War. After the war, Charles trained and worked for many years as a test pilot.

In 1980, NASA selected him as an astronaut candidate. Charles' first spaceflight was on the Space Shuttle *Columbia* on January 12, 1986. He served as the pilot for a crew of seven as they placed a communication **satellite** in space. On April 24, 1990, he would be the pilot for the Space Shuttle *Discovery*. Charles would go into space four times. For his last two spaceflights, he would serve as **commander** on the Space Shuttle *Atlantis* (1992) and the Space Shuttle *Discovery* (1994). Charles retired from NASA in 1994 and returned to the Marine Corps.

In 2009, President Barack Obama was nominated, and the U.S. Senate confirmed Charles Frank Bolden, Jr. to become the 12th NASA administrator.

He would be the first African-American administrator. During his time as administrator, NASA made a big change by stopping the space shuttle program in 2011. While private companies would take on spaceflights, NASA continued to do other projects like landing the Curiosity rover on the planet Mars.

Credits: NASA

A **rover** is a vehicle that is used to drive over a rough terrain. A remote control is used to move the vehicle. Since 2012, five rovers have landed on

Mars. They are called Sojourner, Spirit and Opportunity, Curiosity, and Perseverance.

Charles Bolden served in this position until 2017.

MAE C. JEMISON

1956-

Dr. Mae C. Jemison, an engineer, and a physician, is the first African American female astronaut.

Mae C. Jemison was born in Decatur, Alabama. She is the youngest of three children. As a young girl, Mae spent a lot of time reading and found herself drawn to wanting to learn more about astronomy. **Astronomy** is the study of everything in the universe, like planets, stars, comets, and galaxies.

In 1973, after she graduated from high school, she went to Stanford University on a National Achievement Scholarship. In 1977, she graduated from Stanford University with a degree in chemical engineering. A **chemical engineer** creates and designs processes using chemicals. They often work in a laboratory.

Dr. Jemison later earned a medical degree from Cornell University. During her time working as a doctor in Los Angeles, California, NASA selected her and fourteen others for astronaut training. Dr. Jemison completed her training as a mission specialist with NASA in 1988. She became the first African American female astronaut in 1992 on the Space Shuttle *Endeavor*.

The part of the space shuttle that carried astronauts is known as an orbiter or a spaceplane. They built six orbiters for flight: *Enterprise, Columbia, Challenger, Discovery, Atlantis,* and *Endeavour*. The *Endeavor* was the final orbiter. They built it to replace the *Challenger*, which tragically exploded 73 seconds into its flight, killing the seven crew members on January 28, 1986.

After her historic space flight, Dr. Jemison resigned from NASA in 1993 and founded the Jemison Group, Inc. Among her current projects are several that focus on improving healthcare in Africa. Dr. Jemison worked as a professor of environmental studies at Dartmouth College from 1995 to 2002.

She continues to encourage children to pursue careers in science and has written children's books.

STEPHANIE D. WILSON

1966 -

Stephanie D. Wilson is the second African American woman to go into space after Mae Jemison. She's flown to space onboard three Space Shuttle missions.

Stephanie Denise Wilson was born in Boston, Massachusetts, in 1966. Stephanie's parents exposed her to the world of engineering. Her dad was an **electrical engineer**, a career that involves the study and design of devices, equipment, and systems that use electricity. Her mother worked at Lockheed Martin, a global security and aerospace company.

It was during middle school that Stephanie really learned what she wanted to do when she grew up. She interviewed an **astronomer**, a person who studies everything in the universe like planets, stars, comets, and galaxies.

Stephanie's interest in space grew as she began her journey after graduating from high school. In 1988, she earned a bachelor's degree in engineering science from Harvard University. After graduation, she worked as an engineer for Martin Marietta Astronautics Group in Denver, Colorado. Stephanie returned to school and worked on her Master's degree. In 1992, armed with a master's degree, Stephanie began working at the Jet Propulsion Laboratory in Pasadena, California.

Finally, in April 1996, Stephanie's dream of becoming an astronaut became a reality. She was one of 43 people selected to be an astronaut candidate. There were over 2,500 people who applied! As an astronaut candidate, Stephanie had to train to be inside a space shuttle. Her training took place at the Johnson Space Center, where Stephanie would eventually become a Mission Specialist.

On July 4, 2006, Stephanie made her first journey into space on the Space Shuttle *Discovery*. This was about 14 years after Mae C. Jemison became the first African American female astronaut in space. As of 2021, Stephanie has had 42 days in space, the most of any female African American astronaut.

In 2020, Stephanie became one of 18 astronauts training for the NASA Artemis program. This program is planning to send the first woman and the next man to the moon. On July 21, 1969, Neil Armstrong became the first person to walk on the moon.

The Artemis team includes astronauts Victor Glover and Jessica Watkins too. Their bios come later in this book.

MICHAEL P. ANDERSON

1959-2003

Astronaut Michael P. Anderson died along with his crew of seven when Space Shuttle Columbia disintegrated during re-entry on February 1, 2003.

Michael P. Anderson was born on December 25, 1959, in Plattsburgh, New York. Michael was from a military family who moved around a lot because of his father's career in the Air Force. Michael would follow in his father's footsteps by joining the Air Force ROTC in college.

In 1981, he graduated with degrees in physics and astronomy from the University of Washington in Seattle, Washington. Since he took part in ROTC, he started active service in the Air Force after graduation.

NASA selected Michael for astronaut training in 1995. It would be three years later, in 1998, when he made his first spaceflight in Space Shuttle *Endeavor*. The mission included moving over 9,000 pounds of equipment, hardware, and water from the *Endeavor* to the Russian space station *Mir*. It took the crew a little over eight days to complete the mission.

Michael's second spaceflight was on NASA's oldest space shuttle *Columbia*. For the mission on January 16, 2003, it would be the 28th time the Space Shuttle *Columbia* carried a crew to space. The crew was in space for 16 days and conducted almost 80 experiments for science and research. But something went really wrong when the space shuttle tried to return to Earth for a landing. Michael died along with his crew of seven when *Columbia* broke apart 40 miles from the landing strip on February 1, 2003.

JOAN HIGGINBOTHAM

1964-

Joan Higginbotham, a NASA astronaut and an electrical engineer, is the third African American woman to go into space, after Mae Jemison and Stephanie Wilson.

Joan Elizabeth Higginbotham was born in Chicago, Illinois, on August 3, 1964. After graduating from the Whitney Young Magnet High School in 1982, she attended Southern Illinois University Carbondale. She received a Bachelor of Science with a focus in Electrical Engineering in 1986. Joan would continue her education at the Florida Institute of Technology, where she earned Masters of Science in Management in 1992 and Space Systems in 1996.

In 1987, her career started at NASA as a Payload Electrical Engineer for the Kennedy Space Center in Florida. Over the next nine years, Joan worked on many of the NASA Space Shuttle launches, including *Atlantis* and *Columbia*. In April 1996, NASA selected Joan as an astronaut candidate and reported to Johnson Space Center in Texas. It would still be almost ten years before she went into space.

In December 2006, Joan took her first spaceflight as a mission specialist on Space Shuttle *Discovery*. She became the third African American woman to travel into space after Dr. Mae Jemison and Stephanie D. Wilson. Joan was a part of a seven member crew. The crew's main mission was to continue building the International Space Station (ISS). ISS started on November 20, 1998, when the United States and Russia began working together to learn more about how humans can live in space. For almost 13 days, Joan and her fellow crew members did spacewalks and worked with the ISS's robotic arm to move equipment.

Joan retired from NASA in 2007. She's worked at several private companies and is currently a consultant for Joan Higginbotham Ad Astra, LLC. She continues to speak about her experiences and encourages other women to try STEM careers.

PART 3

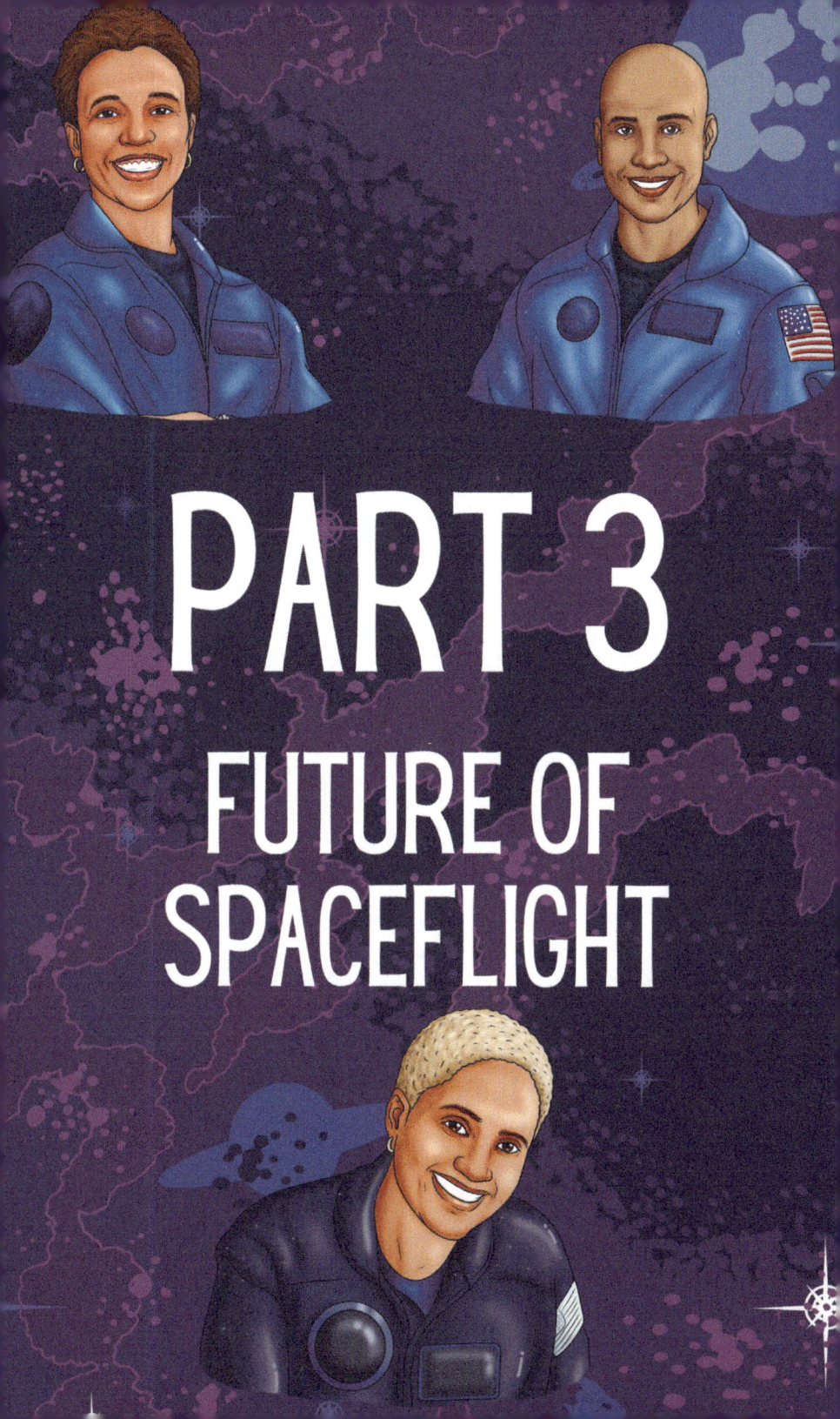

FUTURE OF SPACEFLIGHT

VICTOR GLOVER

1976-

Victor J. Glover, Jr. made history by becoming the first African American astronaut to live on the International Space Station. He also was a pilot for SpaceX Crew Dragon capsule "Resilience."

Victor J. Glover, Jr. was born in Pomona, California, on April 30, 1976. A teacher recognized Victor's love for math and science and encouraged him to pursue engineering. After graduating from Ontario High School in Ontario, California, he attended California Polytechnic State University in San Luis Obispo. In 2013, over 6,400 people had applied for astronaut training. NASA selected Victor to be one of eight members of the 21st NASA astronaut class. Victor would not take his first spaceflight until November 15, 2020. On this mission, he was the pilot and second-in-command for Crew-1 on the **SpaceX** Crew Dragon capsule "Resilience."

Victor played football while pursuing an engineering degree. After a rigorous number of years, he earned his bachelors in 1999. Like many astronauts before him, Victor earned his "wings" and became a pilot in the Navy. While he served in the Navy, he logged 3,000 flight hours in over 40 different aircraft.

Victor made history by becoming the first African American astronaut to live on the **International Space Station (ISS)**. Astronauts have been staying on ISS since November 2000.

Usually, there are seven crew members from all around the world. Their goal is to study and research how humans can live in space. The ISS orbits around the Earth every 90 minutes, traveling at five miles per second. Victor and his crew members remained in space for six months or 168 days. They returned to Earth, landing in the Gulf of Mexico near Panama City, Florida, on May 2, 2021.

NASA selected Victor along with 18 other astronauts for NASA's Artemis team. The Artemis team includes astronauts Stephanie Wilson and Jessica Watkins too. Goals for the Artemis program include the first woman and the first person of color to walk on the moon since the Apollo mission on July 24, 1969.

DR. SIAN PROCTOR

1970-

Dr. Sian Proctor is the first African American woman to pilot a spacecraft and the fourth African American woman in space. Dr. Proctor

was also a part of the first all-civilian crew in space.

Sian Hayley Proctor was born on March 28, 1970, in Hagåtña, Guam. Considered United States territory, Guam is in the western Pacific Ocean, not too far from the Philippines.

As a child, Sian observed her father's love for NASA. He had been a NASA engineer who helped track flights for the Apollo program. One of the important events during the **Apollo program** took place on July 21, 1969, when astronaut Neil Armstrong became the first person to walk on the moon.

Sian took an interest in **Geology**, the study of the Earth and its physical elements. In 1998, she graduated from Arizona State University with a master's degree in Geology. In 2006, she earned a Ph.D. in Science education.

In 2009, the geoscientist hoped to become one of nine astronaut candidates after making it past 3,500 other applicants. NASA didn't select her. Despite not becoming an astronaut, Sian never lost her dream to go to space.

Sian would later become a **commercial** astronaut. This is a different type of astronaut from years past. NASA astronauts worked for the United States government. A commercial astronaut can pilot, command, or be a crew member for privately funded spacecrafts.

Sian took part in the Shift4Shop contest. An entrepreneur and artist, too, she created a shop called "Space2Inspire," where she offers "AfronautSpace" art. Sian won the contest and a seat aboard **Inspiration4**. Inspiration4 is a privately funded trip to Earth's orbit by billionaire Jared Isaacman. The crew of four people included Jared Isaacman, Hayley Arceneaux, Chris Sembroski, and Dr. Sian Proctor.

On September 15, 2021, Sian became the first African American woman to pilot a spacecraft and the fourth African American woman in space.

View her AfronautSpace art at https://myspace2inspire.com/

JESSICA WATKINS

1988-

NASA astronaut Jessica Watkins will be the first African American woman to complete a long-term mission aboard the International Space Station for the SpaceX Crew-4 launch. This will be Jessica's first spaceflight.

Jessica Watkins was born in Gaithersburg, Maryland on May 14, 1988. After graduating from high school, Jessica attended Stanford where she played on the rugby team. Jessica earned a bachelor of science degree in geological and environmental sciences from Stanford University.

She earned a Ph.D. in geology at the University of California, Los Angeles. Jessica researched landslides on both Earth and Mars. Her study of Mars led her to work as a postdoctoral fellow at the California Institute of Technology (CalTech). While at CalTech, she became a member of the team that planned missions for NASA's Curiosity Rover.

In 2017, NASA selected Jessica for astronaut training. She was one of twelve astronaut candidates selected from over 18,300 applicants. In 2022, Jessica will take her first spaceflight on **SpaceX**'s Crew-4 mission. She will be the first African American woman to complete a long-term mission aboard the **International Space Station** (ISS).

Jessica was also selected along with 18 other astronauts for NASA's Artemis team. The Artemis team includes astronauts Victor Glover and Stephanie Wilson too. Goals for the Artemis program include the first woman and the first person of color to walk on the moon since the Apollo mission on July 24, 1969.

Timeline

1940s

1943 - The NACA West Computing Unit started with a group of female African American mathematicians who worked as "human computers."

1949 - **Dorothy Vaughan** became the first African American manager at NASA.

1950s

1958 - The NACA West Computing Unit ended.

1958 - **Mary Jackson** got her degree in aerospace engineering and became NASA's first African American engineer.

1959 - **Melba Roy Mouton** began working for NASA. She served as Head Mathematician on the Echo Project.

1960s

1961 - On May 5, 1961, Alan Shepard would become the first American in space thanks to **Katherine Johnson's** calculations.

1967 - **Christine Darden** started her career at NASA as a human computer.

1967 - **Robert H. Lawrence** became a test pilot at Edwards Air Force Base. While testing a jet plane called a Starfighter, Robert lost his life in December 1967. Recognized now as the first African American astronaut.

1970s

1978 - **Guion Bluford**, **Ronald McNair** and **Fredrick Gregory** were all selected as astronaut candidates. Almost 8,000 people applied to the program, and they were three of thirty-five selected.

1980s

1983 - **Guion Bluford** became the first African American astronaut to travel to space.

1984 - **Dr. Ronald E. McNair** would take his first spaceflight on Space Shuttle *Challenger*. He would be the second African American astronaut in space.

1986 - **Dr. Ronald E. McNair** along with a crew of seven lost their lives in the Space Shuttle *Challenger* disaster.

1988 - **Dr. Mae C. Jemison** completed her training as a mission specialist with NASA.

1990s

1992 - **Dr. Mae C. Jemison** became first African American female astronaut when she flew on the Space Shuttle Endeavor.

1997 - Almost thirty years after his death, NASA finally recognized **Major Robert H. Lawrence, Jr**. as the first African American astronaut.

2000s

2003 - **Michael P. Anderson** died along with his crew of seven when Space Shuttle *Columbia* broke apart 40 miles from the landing strip on February 1, 2003.

2006 - **Stephanie D. Wilson** made her first journey into space on the Space Shuttle *Discovery*, becoming the second African American female astronaut.

2006 - In December 2006, **Joan Higginbotham** took her first spaceflight as a mission specialist on Space Shuttle *Discovery*.

2009 - President Barack Obama nominated and the U.S. Senate confirmed **Charles Frank Bolden, Jr.** to become the 12th NASA administrator. He would be the first African-American administrator.

2020s

2020 - **Stephanie D. Wilson, Victor Glover** and **Jessica Watkins** became three of 18 astronauts training for the NASA Artemis program. Goals for the Artemis program include the first woman and the first person of color to walk on the moon since the Apollo mission on July 24, 1969.

2020-2021 - From November 15, 2021-May 2, 2021, **Victor J. Glover, Jr.** made history by becoming the first African American astronaut to live on the International Space Station.

2021 - On September 15, 2021, **Dr. Sian Proctor** became the first African American woman to pilot a spacecraft and the fourth African American woman in space.

2022 - On April 27, 2022, **Jessica Watkins** took her first spaceflight on SpaceX's Crew-4 mission. She will be the first African American woman to complete a long-term mission aboard the International Space Station (ISS).

Glossary

Several vocabulary words were introduced throughout the book. Below you can find a review of definitions and also how to say the words out loud. Some of these are great words to know if you are ever in a spelling bee!

Aerospace (eh-row-spays) - The study of the earth's atmosphere and space.

Astronomy (uh-straa-nuh-mee) - The study of everything in the universe like planets, stars, comets, and galaxies.

Discrimination (duh-skri-muh-nay-shn) - When people are treated differently and usually not in a very nice way.

Doctorate (daak-tr-uht) - The highest degree a student can earn from a college or university, which is usually a PhD.

Engineer (en-juh-neer) - A person who can design or build some pretty complex things like machines, systems, or structures.

Geology (jee·aa·luh·jee) **-** The study of the earth and its physical elements.

Satellite (sa-tuh-lite) - A body like the moon, planet or object that orbit or moves along a curved path around another planet or a star.

Segregation (seh·gruh·gay·shn) - Setting one group of people apart from another group. Most of the times one group was treated unfairly.

Trajectory (truh-jek-tr-ee) - A path needed for an orbital flight.

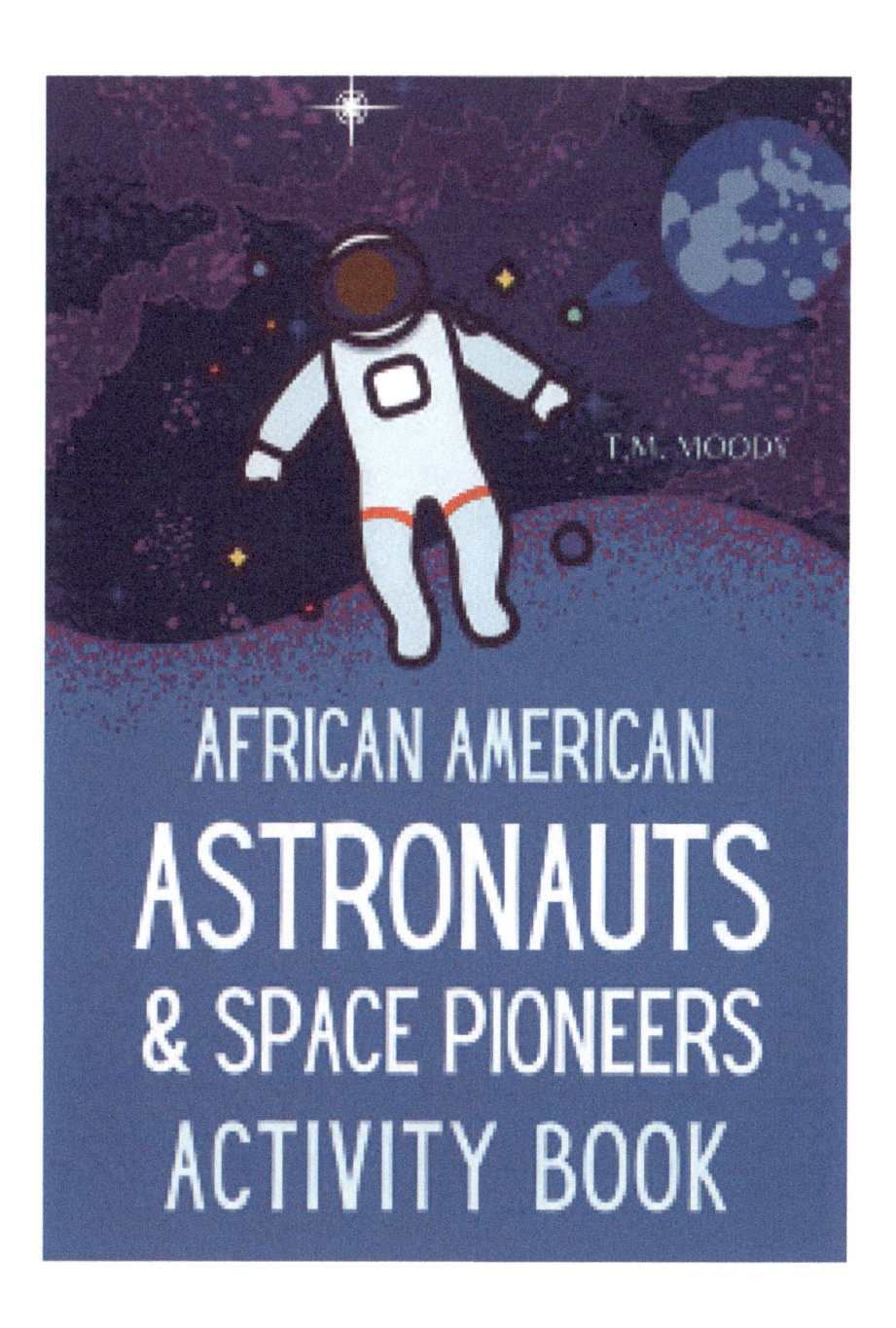

AFRICAN AMERICAN ASTRONAUTS & SPACE PIONEERS ACTIVITY BOOK

T.M. MOODY

Activity Book

Do you like coloring or puzzles? Be sure to check out ***African American Astronauts & Space Pioneers***. The activity book includes over 40 activities like coloring, word search, crossword puzzles, mazes, and more. Download free activity sheets at TheKultureKidz.com.

About the Author

T.M. Moody has a deep love for history and started the Kulture Kidz website in 1999. She has worked over twenty years as an education content creator and digital curator in public media. Her specialty is creating interactive, standards-based content for the K-12 community.

Moody also has been an author for over ten years. She writes mysteries under her real name, Tyora Moody.

Kulture Kidz Books

Kulture Kidz Books creates content and books for ages 6-12. Our mission is to learn about people who made a difference.

For this book's bibliography, visit https://thekulturekidz.com/bibliographies/

Made in the USA
Monee, IL
12 December 2022